SECOND EDITION 1

T0303278

SUPER PRACTICE

Emma Szlachta · Garan Holcombe

CAMBRIDGE
UNIVERSITY PRESS

Map of the book

Unit	Grammar/Language	Reading/Writing	Listening/Speaking
● (pages 4–11)	• Numbers • Colours	A chat	Greetings
1 (pages 12–19)	• Questions and short answers • Imperatives	A comic strip	Classroom objects
2 (pages 20–27)	• *What's his/her …?* *How old is he/she?* • Adjectives	An email	Toys and friends
3 (pages 28–35)	• *in, on, under* • *I like / I don't like …*	A project	Animals
4 (pages 36–43)	• *I've got / I haven't got …* • *Have … got any …?*	A text message	Food
5 (pages 44–51)	• Free time activities • *Do you …? Yes, I do. / No, I don't.*	A blog	Free time activities
6 (pages 52–59)	• *There's / There are …* • *Is there / Are there …? /* *How many …?*	A project	Houses and rooms
7 (pages 60–67)	• *Do you like this/these …?* • *Is he/she + -ing?*	A chat	Clothes
8 (pages 68–75)	• *can/can't* for ability • Questions with *can*	A forum	The body and actions
9 (pages 76–83)	• Suggestions • *Where's / Where are …?*	A magazine	Holidays

Numbers

What's your name?

How old are you?

What's your name?

I'm Ben and I'm seven.

I'm Alice.

I'm seven.

I'm Ned and I'm eight.

Language focus

Use **How old are you?** and **I'm ...** to ask and answer about ages.

How old are you?   ***I'm*** *nine.*

I'm *ten.*

1   **Match the numbers.**

How old are you?

1   I'm seven.

2   I'm five.

3   I'm ten.

4   I'm one.

5   I'm three.

6   I'm nine.

1

9

5

7

3

10

2 Follow the numbers in the maze.

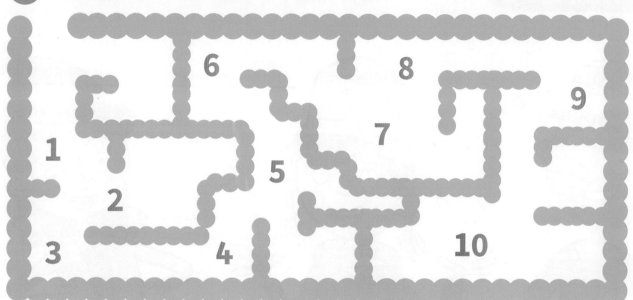

3 Write the numbers.

1
one

2

3

4

5

6

7

8

9

10

Colours

I'm Ned. My hat is blue.

I'm Ben. My hat is green.

What's your name?

Language focus

Use **colours** to describe different objects.

*A **blue** hat.   My hat is **green**.*

1 **Match the colours with the words.**

1 blue

2 orange

3 yellow

4 red

5 green

6 purple

2 **Write the letters to complete the colours.**

1 gr _e_ _e_ n

3 r ___ ___

5 ___ e ___ l ___ w

2 o ___ a ___ ___ e

4 ___ ur ___ l ___

6 b ___ ___ e

3 **Write the colours.**

1 A ___ *blue* ___ balloon.

2 A _____ balloon.

3 A _____ balloon.

4 A _____ balloon.

5 A _____ balloon.

6 An _____ balloon.

Reading: a chat

1 Read the conversation and match the phrases.

Sally Green

Hi! I'm Sally. What's your name?

Hugo Black

I'm Hugo. How old are you?

Sally Green

I'm eight. How old are you?

Hugo Black

I'm seven.

1 Sally   a seven
2 Hugo   b Green
3 Sally is   c eight
4 Hugo is   d Black

1 **Write the questions.**

1 you / old / How / are / ?

_____

2 your / name / What's / ?

_____

2 **Write a chat with a friend. Draw pictures.**

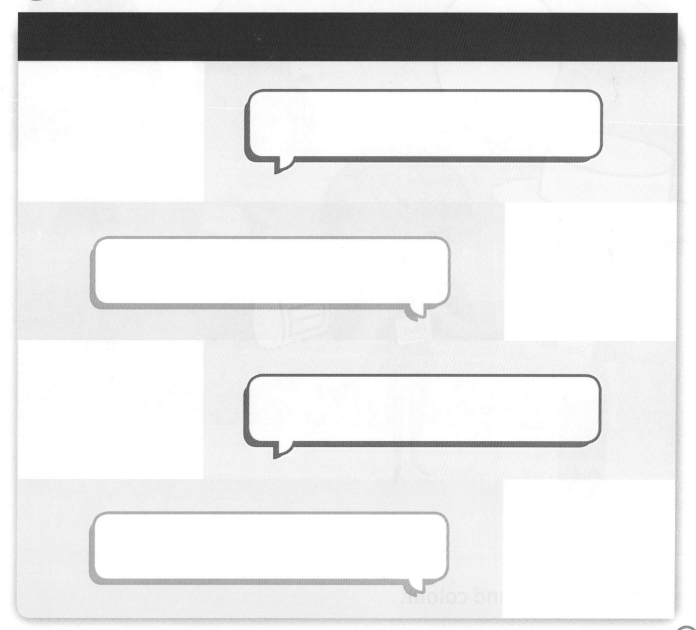

Listening: greetings

1 🎧 01 **Listen and draw lines.**

6   7   8   9

2 🎧 02 **Listen and colour.**

1 Draw a picture of you with a hat and a balloon.

2 Look at your picture and write answers. Then practise.

1 What's your name?   I'm _____.

2 How old are you?   I'm _____.

3 What colour is your hat?   My hat is _____.

4 What colour is your balloon?   My balloon is _____.

3 Work with a friend. Ask and answer.

Hi! I'm Tom. What colour is your hat?

Hello! I'm Lucy. My hat is orange.

1 Questions and short answers

Language focus

Use **What's this?** to ask about objects and **It's a ...** to answer.
Use **Is it ... ?** to ask about objects and **No, it isn't / Yes, it is** to give short answers.

What's this? ***It's a*** pencil.   ***Is it*** a pen? ***No, it isn't. / Yes, it is.***

---

1 Look at the pictures. Match the questions with the responses.

1 Is it a rubber?

2 Is it a pencil?

3 Is it a desk?

4 Is it a pencil case?

5 Is it a ruler?

6 Is it a bag?

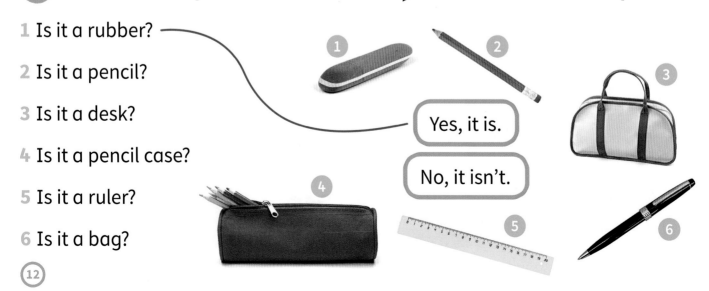

2 Match the questions with the responses.

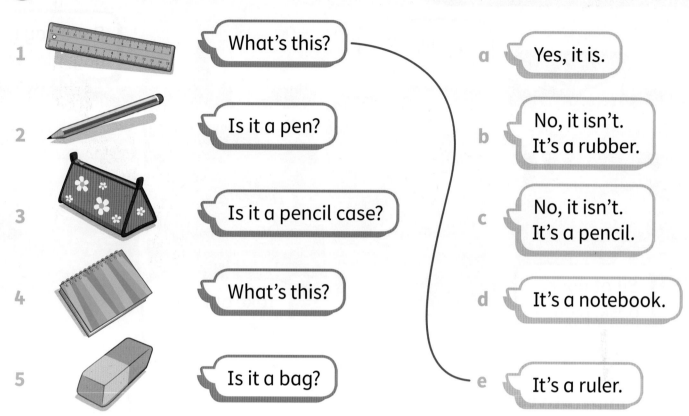

1   What's this?   a   Yes, it is.

2   Is it a pen?   b   No, it isn't.
                                                          It's a rubber.

3   Is it a pencil case?   c   No, it isn't.
                                                          It's a pencil.

4   What's this?   d   It's a notebook.

5   Is it a bag?   e   It's a ruler.

3 Write questions and answers.

1 this / What's / ?

What's this?

a / It's / desk / .

_____

2 rubber / it / Is / a / ?

_____

is / Yes, / it / .

_____

3 it / notebook / Is / a / ?

_____

isn't / it / No, / .

_____

4 this / What's / ?

_____

a / It's / bag / green / .

_____

5 this / What's / ?

_____

a / desk / yellow / It's / .

_____

Imperatives

> Open your bag, please.

> Put away your bag, please.

> Sit at your desk, please.

> Take out your pen, please.

Language focus

Use **imperatives** to give instructions.

Open your book, please.

Sit at your desk, please.

Put away your book, please.

Pass me a ruler, please.

Close your bag, please.

Take out your ruler, please.

1 Match the sentences with the pictures.

1 Close your bag, please. **b**

2 Pass me a ruler, please. ☐

3 Take out your book, please. ☐

4 Pass me a pen, please. ☐

5 Take out your ruler, please. ☐

6 Open your bag, please. ☐

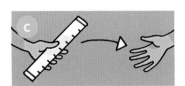
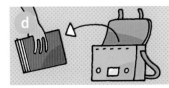

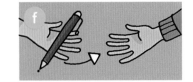

2 **Complete the sentences with the words from the box.**

Put   Turn   Pass   Open   away   ~~Pass~~

1  ___Pass___ me a pencil, please.

2  _____ your books, please.

3  _____ around.

4  _____ your rubber on your head.

5  _____ me a ruler, please.

6  Put _____ your bags, please.

3 **Look and write.**

1 Open ___your bags___, please.

2 Sit at _____.

3 Close _____, please.

4 Pass _____, please.

5 Take _____, please.

6 Put _____, please.

1 **Read the text and draw lines.**

1 What objects are on your desk and in your classroom?

a black book _____ _____ _____

_____ _____ _____ _____

2 Write a story. Draw pictures.

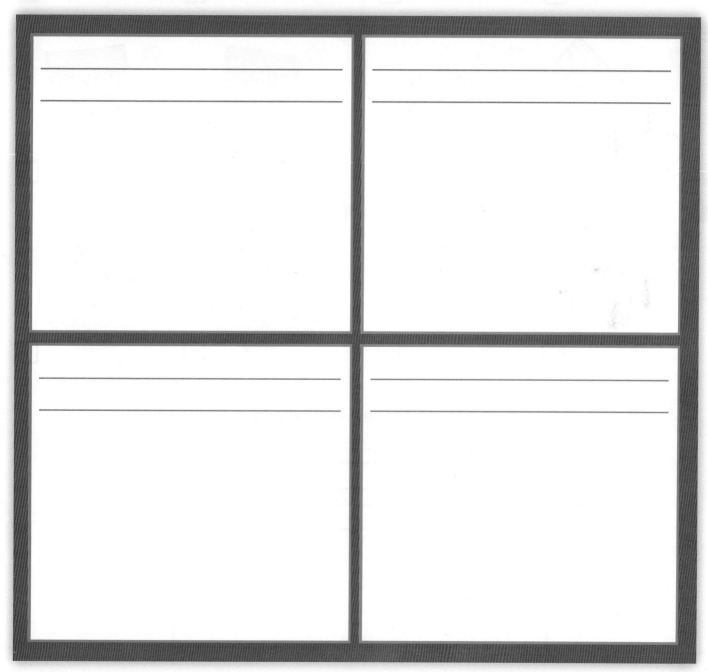

1 🎧 03 Listen and tick ☑ the correct picture.

2 🎧 04 Look at the box. Listen and do the actions.

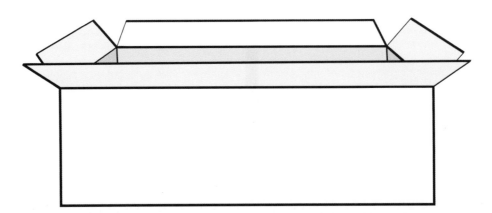

1 Look and write. Then ask and answer.

> What's letter 'a'?

> It's a pen.

a

b

c

d

pen

2 Draw three classroom objects.

3 Work with a friend. Talk about your classroom objects.

> What's this?

> It's my pencil case. It's orange.

2 What's his/her ... ? How old is he/she?

Language focus

Asking and answering questions using **his**, **her**, **he** and **she**.

*What's **his** name?*	***His** name's Ned.*
*How old is **he**?*	***He**'s six.*
*What's **his** favourite toy?*	***His** favourite toy's his ball.*
*What's **her** name?*	***Her** name's Alice.*
*How old is **she**?*	***She**'s eight.*
*What's **her** favourite toy?*	***Her** favourite toy's her kite.*

1 Match the questions with the responses.

1 What's her name?
2 What's her favourite toy?
3 How old is she?
4 What's his favourite toy?
5 What's his name?
6 How old is he?

a He's ten.
b His name's Tim.
c Her name's Kim.
d She's six.
e Her favourite toy's her bike.
f His favourite toy's his plane.

2 Complete the sentences with the words from the box.

favourite ~~her~~ She's What's name she

1 What's **her** name?

Her _____'s Sophie.

2 _____ her favourite toy?

Her _____ toy's her go-kart.

3 How old is _____?

_____ seven.

3 Write questions and answers.

1 his / What's / name / ?

What's his name?

Ben / His / name's / .

_____

2 Toby / How / old / is / ?

_____

seven / He's / .

_____

3 his / What's / number / favourite / ?

_____

number / favourite / is / His / ten / .

_____

4 her / What's / name / ?

_____

name's / Mary / Her / .

_____

Adjectives

It's a big yellow plane.

It's a long red train.

It's a new black go-kart.

It's an ugly orange monster!

Language focus

Use **an** before words beginning with **a**, **e**, **i**, **o** or **u** (vowels).

It's *a new* kite.   It's *an ugly* monster.

It's *a long blue* train.   It's *a big green* ball.

---

1 Look, read and tick ☑ or cross ☒.

1 It's a long red train. ☒
2 It's a big green ball. ☐
3 It's an ugly blue monster. ☐
4 It's a new pink go-kart. ☐
5 It's a long blue train. ☐
6 It's a big yellow ball. ☐

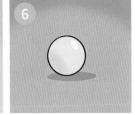

2 Circle the correct words to complete the sentences.

1 It's *(a)* / *an* short green train.

2 It's *a* / *an* ugly purple monster.

3 It's a *beautiful new* / *new beautiful* doll.

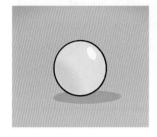  

4 It's *a* / *an* small yellow ball.

5 It's a *green big* / *big green* monster.

6 It's *a* / *an* old black go-kart.

3 Write sentences with *a/an* and the words from the box.

> ~~yellow bike~~   ugly green monster   yellow and red plane
> beautiful doll   blue car   big ball

1 It's **a yellow bike**. 2 It's _____. 3 It's _____.

4 It's _____. 5 It's _____. 6 It's _____.

Reading: an email

1 **Read the text and answer the questions.**

● ● ●

To: Ana

From: Tom

Hi, Ana

I'm Tom and I'm seven. My favourite toy's my yellow go-kart. It's new! Look – this is my go-kart!

What's your favourite toy? How old are you?

Tom

● ● ●

To: Tom

From: Ana

Hi, Tom

I'm seven. My favourite toy isn't a doll or a computer game. My favourite toy's my bike. It's a new green bike. My favourite colour's green. Look – this is my bike! What's your favourite colour?

Ana

1 What's his name?

His name's Tom.

2 How old is he?

_____

3 What's his favourite toy?

_____

4 What's her name?

_____

5 What colour is her bike?

_____

6 What's her favourite colour?

_____

1 **Write answers.**

What's your favourite toy? _____

What colour is it? _____

Is it new or old? _____

What isn't your favourite toy? _____

2 **Write an email to Tom or Ana. Use your notes from Activity 1. Draw a picture of the toy.**

● ● ●

To:

From:

Listening: toys and friends

1 🎧 **05** Listen and number the pictures.

a

b

c

d

2 🎧 **06** Listen and colour.

1 **Talk about the toys. Use the words.**

> Number 1 is a small pink monster.

1

2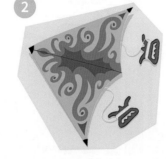

3

4

small pink   beautiful green   new orange   big red

2 **Look at the toys in Activity 1. Play the guessing game.**

> It's new and orange. What is it?

> It's the go-kart.

3 **Look at Activity 1 and choose a toy for a friend. Then write and say.**

My friend's name is _____. He's/She's _____.
This toy is for my friend. It's a _____.

> My friend's name is Luc. He's six. This toy is for my friend. It's a big red ball.

3 in, on, under

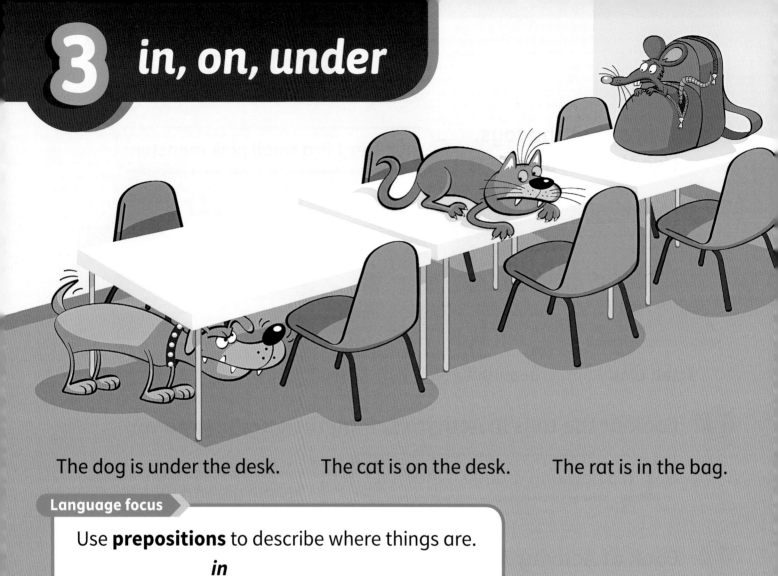

The dog is under the desk.   The cat is on the desk.   The rat is in the bag.

Language focus

Use **prepositions** to describe where things are.

	in	
The lizard is	***on***	*the bag.*
	under	

1 **Match the sentences with the pictures.**

1 The cat is under the desk.   b

2 The frog is in the bag.   ☐

3 The lizard is on the bag.   ☐

4 The lizard is in the pencil case.   ☐

5 The rat is under the desk.   ☐

2 Write *in*, *on* or *under*. Draw lines.

1 The rats are __**in**__ the desk.

2 The ducks are _____ the books.

3 The elephants are _____ the ruler.

4 The cats are _____ the desk.

5 The lizards are _____ the bag.

6 The spiders are _____ the pencil case.

3 Look and write.

1 The spider is in the pencil case. _____

2 _____

3 _____

4 _____

5 _____

I like / I don't like ...

Language focus

Use **like** and **don't like** to express likes and dislikes.

☺ I **like** dogs.   ☺ I **like** dogs, too.

☹ I **don't like** dogs.

1 Circle the correct words to complete the sentences.

1 I *like* / *don't like* dogs.

2 I *like* / *don't like* ducks.

3 I *like* / *don't like* cats.

4 I *like* / *don't like* frogs.

5 I *like* / *don't like* rats.

2 Complete the sentences with the words from the box.

| too | like | green | ~~like~~ | don't | lizards |

Ben I (1) __*like*__ dogs.

Tim I like dogs, (2) _____ .

Ben I (3) _____ like rats. What about you?

Tim I like rats and I (4) _____ lizards.

Ben I like (5) _____ , too – they are my favourite – big (6) _____ lizards!

3 Look and write.

 ☺

1 I *like cats.*

 ☹

2 _____

 ☺

3 _____

 ☹

4 _____

 ☺

5 _____

 ☹

6 _____

Reading: a project

1 **Look at the pictures. Read the texts and choose *yes* or *no*.**

This is my cat. His name is Felix. He's nine.
His favourite toy's his doll. Felix is a small
brown and black cat. He's in my bag!
I like cats – cats are my favourite.
I don't like dogs. What about you?

Sophie

This is my rat. Her name is Rita.
She's five. Her favourite toy's her ball.
Rita is a small white rat. I like rats –
rats are my favourite. I don't like
cats. What about you?

Max

1 Felix is a rat.   *yes /* (*no*)

2 Felix's favourite toy is his doll.   *yes / no*

3 Felix is on the bag.   *yes / no*

4 Rita is five.   *yes / no*

5 Her favourite toy is her doll.   *yes / no*

6 She is black and white.   *yes / no*

① **Write the sentences.**

1 nine / is / years / old / Digby / .

_____

2 is / white / He / .

_____

3 ball / favourite / His / toy's / his / .

_____

② **Write about Digby. Use the sentences from Activity 1.**

1 🎧 07 **Listen and circle. Then draw the animals.**

① 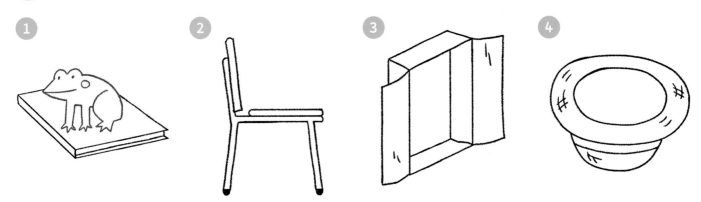 ② ③ ④

1 The frog's (on) / *under* the notebook.

2 The duck's *on* / *under* the chair.

3 The spider's *in* / *on* the box.

4 The cat's *in* / *under* the hat.

2 🎧 08 **Listen and tick ☑ or cross ☒.**

Animals	Jill	Bill
①	✓	✗
②		
③		
④		
⑤		

1 **Find and circle six animals. Then play the memory game.**

Where is the frog?

It's on the ball.

2 **Talk about the animals. Draw 😊 or 😞 for you and your friend.**

I like elephants. What about you?

I don't like elephants.

 😊 Me

😞 My friend

 ◯ Me

◯ My friend

 ◯ Me

◯ My friend

 ◯ Me

◯ My friend

3 **Work with your friend from Activity 2. Say.**

Hi! I'm Tim. I like elephants and cats. Cats are my favourite! I don't like spiders and I don't like lizards.

Hello! I'm Eva. I like …

4 I've got / I haven't got ...

I've got a cheese sandwich.

I haven't got a cheese sandwich.

I've got a cake.

I haven't got a cake.

I've got an apple.

Me too! I've got a big green apple.

Language focus

Use **have got** and **haven't got** to talk about possessions.

I've got a sandwich and an apple.

I haven't got a cake.

1 Look and write *yes* or *no*.

1 I've got a cake.   yes

2 I've got bananas.   ____

3 I've got pizza.   ____

4 I haven't got peas.   ____

5 I haven't got chicken.   ____

6 I've got orange juice.   ____

2 **Complete the sentences with the words from the box.**

| Me | got | too | ~~got~~ | 've | haven't |

1 I've **got** a kiwi.   Me too!

2 I've got pizza.   I _____ got pizza. I've got chicken.

3 I've got a cake.   Me _____ !

4 What's for lunch?   I haven't _____ chicken. I've got sausages.

5 I've got meatballs and peas.   I _____ got meatballs, but I haven't got peas. I've got carrots.

6 I've got a cheese sandwich.   _____ too!

3 **Look and write.**

1 I haven't got a cake.   2 _____

3 _____   4 _____

Have ... got any ... ?

Have we got any cheese?

No, we haven't.

Have we got any cake?

No, we haven't.

Have we got any sausages?

No, we haven't.

Hooray! I like pizza.

Language focus

Use **Have ... got any ... ?** to ask about possessions.
Use **Yes, we have** and **No, we haven't** to give short answers.

Have we *got any* cheese?   *Yes, we have.*
    No, we haven't.

---

1 **Look at the pictures. Match the questions with the responses.**

1 Have we got any apples?

2 Have we got any bananas?

3 Have we got any orange juice?

4 Have we got any sausages?

5 Have we got any cheese?

6 Have we got any chicken?

Yes, we have.   No, we haven't.

2 **Write the dialogue in the correct order.**

> Have you got sausage on your pizza?

> Me too! I like sausages.

> No, I haven't. I don't like carrots. I've got cheese.

> Yes, I have. I've got cheese and sausage. Sausage is my favourite.

> Have you got carrots on your pizza?

Alice **Have you got carrots on your pizza?**

Katy _____

Alice _____

Katy _____

Alice _____

3 **Write questions.**

1 **Have we got any apples?** 2 _____

3 _____ 4 _____

5 _____ 6 _____

Reading: a text message

1 Read. Tick ☑ the food in the text messages.

sausages ☑   steak ☐   chicken ☐   pizza ☐
carrots ☐   peas ☐   bananas ☐   apples ☐
cheese ☐   apple juice ☐   orange juice ☐   milk ☐

7.05 pm

Hi, May! I'm at the shop. I haven't got my shopping list. Look in the kitchen and help me, please! Have we got any cheese?

Hi, Mum!
Yes, we have.

OK. Have we got any bananas and apples?

We've got one banana.
We haven't got any apples.

Have we got any chicken?

No. We haven't got chicken, but we've got eight sausages and we haven't got pizza – pizza's my favourite!

OK, May! A cheese pizza, too!

2 Look at Activity 1. Write the food words.

We haven't got any (1) **apples** , but we've got one (2) _____
and we've got (3) _____ . We haven't got any (4) _____ or
(5) _____ , but we've got eight (6) _____ .

1 **Look and write the food.**

cheese

_____   _____

_____   _____

_____   _____

2 **Look. Write a dialogue about the picture in Activity 1.**

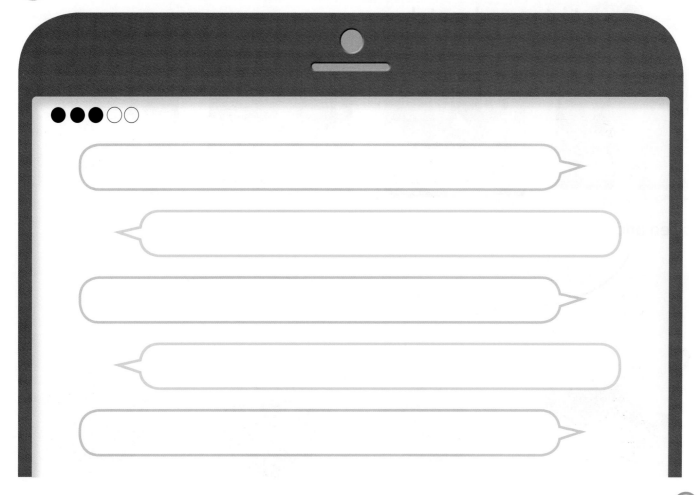

Listening: food

1 🎧 09 Listen and tick ☑ Laura's birthday food.

1 ☑

2 ☐

3 ☐

4 ☐

5 ☐

6 ☐

7 ☐

8 ☐

2 🎧 10 Listen and match.

Leo and Rose

Mum and Nick

Ann and Jack

Dad and Tina

a

b

c

d

1 **What's in your fridge? Draw five things and say.**

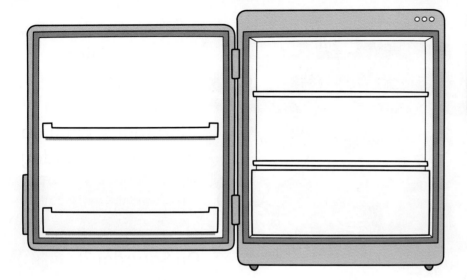

I've got four carrots, six bananas …

2 **Ask a friend about their fridge. Tick ☑ or cross ☒.**

cheese ☐	fish ☐
apples ☐	peas ☐
pizza ☐	carrots ☐
sausages ☐	bananas ☐
chicken ☐	cake ☐
steak ☐	

Have you got any cheese?

Yes, I have. Have you got any cheese?

No, I haven't.

3 **With your friend, look at your fridges in Activity 1. Have you got the same things?**

We've got bananas and sausages.

5 Free time activities

On Thursdays, I play football. What about you?

I go to school on Saturdays.

It's OK. School is cool.

I go swimming on Thursdays. I play football on Saturdays. What do you do on Saturdays?

On Saturday?!

Language focus

Use the verbs **go …** and **play …** to talk about free time activities.
*I **go swimming** on Mondays.*   *I **play football** on Saturdays.*

---

1 **Match the sentences with the pictures.**

1 On Mondays, I ride my bike. ☑ d

2 On Fridays, I play computer games. ☐

3 I go swimming on Thursdays. ☐

4 'What do you do on Sundays?'
'I watch TV and sleep!' ☐

5 I play football with friends on Saturdays. ☐

6 On Tuesdays, I play with my toys. ☐

2 Circle the correct words to complete the sentences.

1 I (play) / go football on Saturdays.

2 I play / go swimming on Fridays.

3 What do you do / go on Thursdays?

4 I ride / play my pony on Sundays.

5 I do / play computer games on Tuesdays.

6 I do / play the piano on Wednesdays.

3 Write sentences with the words from the boxes and days.

go   play   ride   watch

~~football~~   computer games   swimming   TV   ball   bike

1 I play football on Tuesdays.

2 _____

3 _____

4 _____

5 _____

6 _____

Tuesday

Monday

Saturday

Thursday

Friday

Sunday

Do you ... ? Yes, I do. / No, I don't.

Do you watch TV at the weekend?

Yes, I do.

Do you play computer games at the weekend?

No, I don't.

Language focus

Use **Do you ... ?** to ask about activities. Use **Yes, I do** and **No, I don't** to give short answers.

Do you watch TV at the weekend?
No, I don't.

Do you play in the park at the weekend?
Yes, I do.

1 Write *Yes, I do* or *No, I don't*.

1 Do you watch TV at the weekend? ✗ No, I don't.

2 Do you play with your toys on Sundays? ✓ _____

3 Do you play football at the weekend? ✗ _____

4 Do you ride your bike on Tuesdays? ✓ _____

5 Do you play in the park at the weekend? ✓ _____

6 Do you go swimming on Fridays? ✗ _____

2   **Match the sentences with the pictures.**

1 Do you watch TV at the weekend?   [c]

  Yes, I do.

2 Do you play computer games on Fridays?   ☐

  Yes, I do.

3 Do you play computer games at the weekend?   ☐

  No, I don't. I play football.

4 Do you watch TV on Sundays?   ☐

  No, I don't. I read a book.

5 Do you play hide-and-seek at the weekend?   ☐

  No, I don't. I sing with my friends.

6 Do you play football on Sundays?   ☐

  Yes, I do.

3   **Write the questions.**

1 ride / Do / you / at the weekend / your / bike / ?

  Do you ride your bike at the weekend?

2 Do / football / you / on Sundays / play / ?

  _____

3 go / you / at the weekend / swimming / Do / ?

  _____

4 you / hide-and-seek / play / on Saturdays / Do / ?

  _____

5 watch / at the weekend / you / Do / TV / ?

  _____

6 Do / the piano / play / you / on Mondays / ?

  _____

Reading: a blog

1 **Read the blog. Write Sam's diary.**

MyBlog

Sam Brown

My week

It's a busy week for me! On Monday, I play tennis for one hour and on Tuesday, I swim for one hour. On Wednesday and Friday, I watch TV and read a book. On Thursday, I ride my bike with my friend Meg – we ride our bikes for two hours. Saturday is my favourite day! I go to the park and play with my friends – we play football. On Sunday, I watch TV and play computer games. What do you do at the weekend?

Monday	Friday
play tennis	
Tuesday	Saturday
Wednesday	Sunday
Thursday	

1 **Write your diary.**

Monday	Friday
play tennis	
Tuesday	Saturday
Wednesday	Sunday
Thursday	

2 **Write a blog. Use your diary in Activity 1 to help you.
Draw your picture.**

MyBlog

Listening: free time activities

1 🎧 11 **Listen and draw lines.**

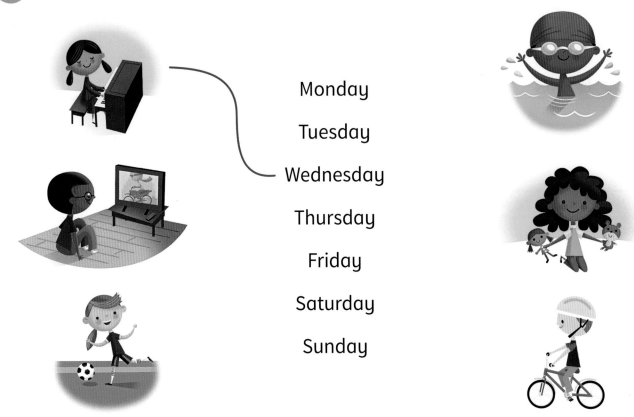

Monday

Tuesday

Wednesday

Thursday

Friday

Saturday

Sunday

2 🎧 12 **Look at Jane's diary. Listen and circle the correct activities.**

Weekend diary

| Friday | go swimming |
| | play tennis |

Saturday	go swimming
	play computer games
	play board games

| Sunday | play football |
| | ride my bike |

1 **Look and do the actions. Play the guessing game.**

> Number 3! You play computer games.

2 **Draw a picture of you on your favourite day. Complete and practise.**

My favourite day is _____. I _____ and _____ on _____.

3 **Talk about your favourite day.**

> My favourite day is Friday. I play football and ride my bike on Fridays.

Friday

6 There's / There are ...

There's a frog under the log.

Cool!

There are two beautiful butterflies on the flower.

Cool!

There's a big scary spider in the tree.

There's ... a monster under the table. Aagh! Oh, it's Spot!

Language focus

Use **there's** and **there are** to say what singular and plural nouns you can see.

There's *a monster.*   **There are** *four cats.*

There's *a frog.*   **There are** *three apples on the tree.*

---

1 Match the words with the pictures.

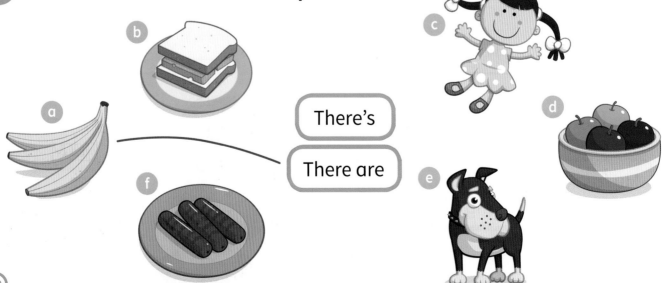

There's

There are

2 **Write *There's* or *There are*.**

1 __There's__ a cat in the living room.

2 _____ five frogs in my bedroom.

3 _____ a cat on the TV.

4 _____ a frog in my bedroom.

5 _____ a monster under the table.

6 _____ two cats in the dining room.

3 **Look and write.**

1 <u>There's a snake in the cellar.</u>

(a snake / cellar)

2 _____ .

(a lizard / bedroom)

3 _____ .

(seven crocodiles / bathroom)

4 _____ .

(five tigers / garden)

5 _____ .

(a spider / kitchen)

6 _____ .

(a cat / living room)

Is there / Are there ...? / How many ...?

Language focus

Use **Is there ... ?** to ask about singular nouns. Use **Are there ... ?** to ask about plural nouns. Use **Yes, there is** and **No, there isn't** to give short answers about singular nouns. Use **Yes, there are** and **No, there aren't** to give short answers about plural nouns.

Use **How many ... are there?** to ask about a plural number of things. Use **There are ...** to give an answer about plural nouns.

Is there a plane?	*Yes, there is.*
Are there any rats?	*No, there aren't.*
How many cars *are there*?	*There are* four cars.

---

1 Circle the correct words to complete the sentences.

1 *Are* / *Is* there any pears?

2 *Are* / *Is* there any rats?

3 How many cars *are* / *is* there?

4 *Are* / *Is* there a plane?

5 *Are* / *Is* there a go-kart?

6 How many cakes *are* / *is* there?

② Look and write answers.

1 Is there a cat? <u>Yes, there is.</u>

2 Are there any balls? _____

3 Is there a frog? _____

4 How many sausages are there? _____

5 Is there a go-kart? _____

6 How many apples are there? _____

 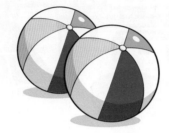 

③ Look. Complete the questions and answers.

1 <u>Are there any</u> bikes? <u>Yes, there are.</u>

2 _____ cars? Yes, _____.

3 _____ are there? _____ eight kites.

4 _____ a plane? _____.

5 _____ a park? _____.

6 _____ are there? _____ one cake.

1 Read the text and the sentences. Write *yes* or *no*.

I live in a big house. It isn't old, it's new. There are four bedrooms, a kitchen, a dining room, a living room and a hall. My bedroom is my favourite room. It's blue. There are posters of animals and I've got a green rug. There's a desk in my bedroom and I've got a computer. There isn't a TV. My toys are in my bedroom and there's a teddy bear. I play with my toys at the weekend.

1 The house is small.   <u>no</u>

2 There are five bedrooms.   _____

3 The rug is blue.   _____

4 There isn't a computer.   _____

5 There's a TV in the bedroom.   _____

6 There are toys in the bedroom.   _____

1 **Make notes about your house and bedroom.**

Rooms | My bedroom | Adjectives

_____ | _____ | _____

_____ | _____ | _____

_____ | _____ | _____

2 **Draw and write about your house and your bedroom.**

_____

_____

_____

_____

_____

_____

_____

1 🎧 13 **Listen and number the rooms.**

2 🎧 14 **Listen to Amy. Circle the correct answers about her house.**

1 How many rooms are there?
  a There are seven rooms.
  (b) There are eight rooms.

2 How many bedrooms are there?
  a There are two bedrooms.
  b There are three bedrooms.

3 Is there a garden?
  a Yes, there is.
  b No, there isn't.

4 Is there a desk in the living room?
  a Yes, there is.
  b No, there isn't.

5 Are there any stairs?
  a Yes, there are.
  b No, there aren't.

1 **Find and circle six differences. Then say.**

There's a yellow ball.

Bedroom A!

2 **Look at the bedrooms in Activity 1. Play the memory game.**

How many pencils are there in Bedroom A?

There are …

Where is the teddy in Bedroom B?

It's …

What colour's … ?

It's …

3 **Choose a bedroom from Activity 1. Talk about it.**

This is Bedroom A. There's a yellow ball. It's on the chair. There are two red books. There are …

7 Do you like this/these ... ?

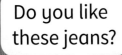

Do you like these jeans?

Yes, I do!

Do you like these shoes?

No, I don't! Put on these shoes.

Do you like this jacket?

No, I don't! Put on this jacket.

Do you like this hat?

Yes, I do!

Language focus

Use **Do you like this ... ?** to ask about singular nouns.
Use **Do you like these ... ?** to ask about plural nouns.
Use **Yes, I do** and **No, I don't** to give short answers.

Do you like this hat?	*Yes, I do.*
Do you like these shoes?	*No, I don't.*

1 Match the words with the pictures.

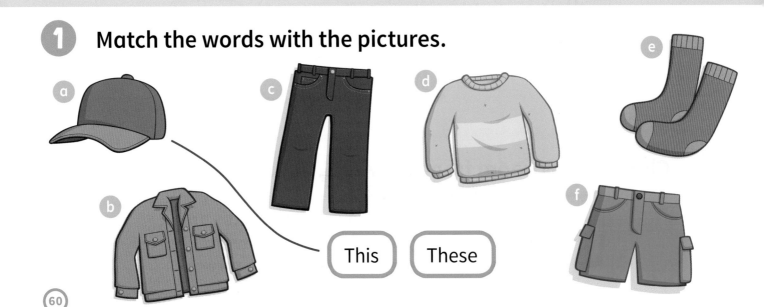

This   These

2 Write the questions.

1 this / Do / like / hat / you / ?   Do you like this hat?

2 these / you / shoes / Do / like / ? _____

3 like / jacket / you / this / Do / ? _____

4 like / you / shorts / these / Do / ? _____

5 T-shirt / Do / you / like / this / ? _____

6 you / jeans / like / Do / these / ? _____

3 Look and write.

1 Do you ____like this hat____ ?
😊 Yes, _____I do_____ .

2 Do you _____ ?
☹ No, _____ .

3 Do you _____ ?
☹ No, _____ .

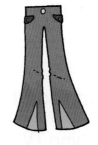

4 Do _____ ?
😊 _____ .

5 Do _____ ?
☹ _____ .

6 _____ ?
😊 _____ .

61

Is he/she + -ing?

Where's James? Is he playing football?

Yes, he is.

That's James.

Is he wearing a black sweater?

No, he isn't. He's wearing a blue sweater.

Oh yes! I can see him.

Language focus

Use **Is he/she + -ing** to ask what people are doing. Use **Yes, he is** and **No, she isn't** to give short answers. Use **is + -ing** to describe what people are doing.

Is he wearing a blue T-shirt?   *Yes, he is.*

Is she wearing brown shoes?   *No, she isn't.*

Olivia's wearing a red sweater.

①   Look and read the questions. Write *yes* or *no*.

1 Is Emma watching TV?   ___yes___

2 Is Paul playing a game?   _____

3 Is Lara singing?   _____

4 Is Ken playing a game?   _____

5 Is Emma wearing a green T-shirt?   _____

6 Is Ken wearing a blue sweater?   _____

2 Write *Yes, he/she is* or *No, he/she isn't.*

1 Is he wearing
red shorts?
<u>Yes, he is.</u>

2 Is he watching TV?
_____

3 Is he wearing a
red sweater?
_____

4 Is she eating cake?
_____

5 Is he playing
football?
_____

6 Is she playing
computer games?
_____

3 Write the questions and sentences.

1 Anna / wearing / is / a blue skirt / .
<u>Anna is wearing a blue skirt.</u>

2 is / What / doing / Bob / ?
_____

3 Are / Amy and Hannah / bikes / riding / ?
_____

4 are / TV / watching / Emma and Tom / .
_____

5 playing / Oscar / football / is / .
_____

6 a sandwich / Kylie / Is / eating / ?
_____

Reading: a chat

1 Read the conversation and answer the questions.

CHATS School friends   *James, Amy*

James Brown   **Amy Little**

Hi, Amy!

I'm in my bedroom. I'm listening to music with my cat! He's on my bed!

Is he sleeping?

Yes, he is.

Where are your mum and brother Luke?

My mum's in the dining room and Luke's in the living room.

Is your mum eating?

No, she isn't. She's reading a book in her favourite chair!

1 Who is James talking to?
   He's talking to Amy.

2 What is the cat doing?
   _____

3 What is James doing?
   _____

4 Where is Mum?
   _____

5 Where is Luke?
   _____

6 Is Mum watching TV?
   _____

1 **Make notes.**

You are at home. What are you doing?

_____

What is your mum doing? Where is she?

_____

Have you got a cat or a dog? What is he/she doing?

_____

What is your brother/sister doing? Where is he/she?

_____

2 **Write a conversation with your friend.**

CHATS School friends

_____

_____

_____

_____

_____

_____

_____

Listening: clothes

1 🎧 15 Listen and draw 😃 or 😞.

1

2

3

4

5

6

2 🎧 16 Listen and match.

1 Stan

2 Oscar

3 Stella

4 Lucy

5 Maya

a

b

c

d

e

1 **Play the description game. Use the words.**

Bob

Bob's wearing a yellow T-shirt and blue shorts. He's playing tennis.

Helen

T-shirt
shorts
cap
football

Matt

sweater
trousers
shoes
TV

Pat

jacket
skirt
banana

Bob

T-shirt
shorts
tennis

2 **Draw a picture of you wearing your favourite clothes. Talk about your picture.**

In this picture, I'm wearing my favourite clothes. I'm wearing …

3 **Show your picture to a friend. Ask and answer.**

Do you like this T-shirt?

Yes, I do! Do you like these jeans?

I can skip.

I can't skip.

I can touch my toes.

I can't touch my toes.

I can stand on one leg.

I can stand on one leg.

And I can stand on one leg, too!

Language focus

Use **can** and **can't** to talk about ability.

I **can** stand on one leg.   I **can't** touch my toes.

She **can** skip.   He **can't** skip.

1   **Match the sentences with the pictures.**

1 He can't swim.   [f]

2 He can play football.   ☐

3 He can skip.   ☐

4 She can stand on one leg.   ☐

5 She can't play the piano.   ☐

6 She can't ride a bike.   ☐

2 Write *can* or *can't*.

1   ✗ He __can't__ swim.

2   ✓ He _____ ride a horse.

3   ✗ She _____ play tennis.

4   ✗ He _____ play the piano.

5   ✓ She _____ ride a bike.

6   ✓ She _____ do ballet.

3 Look and write.

	Ned	Alice
🎹	✗	✓
Hola	✗	✓
🎸	✓	✗

1   Ned can't play the piano.

2   _____

3   _____

4   _____

5   _____

6   _____

Questions with *can*

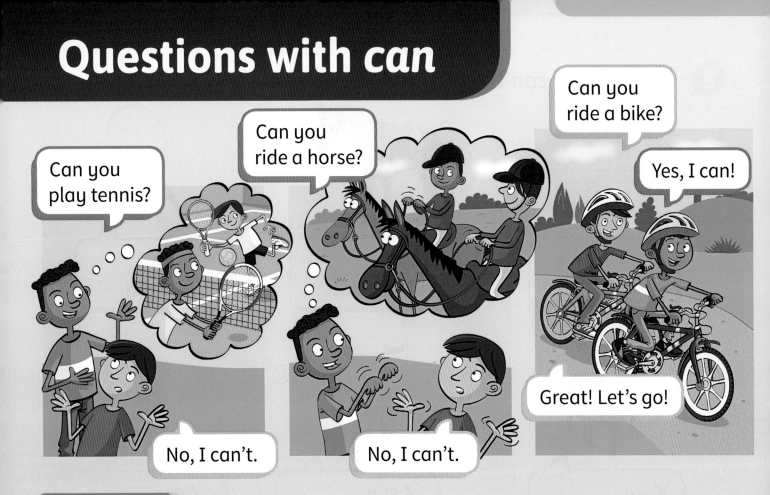

Language focus

Use **can** to ask about ability. Use **Yes, I can** and **No, I can't** to give short answers.

Can you swim?	**Yes, I can.**
Can you dance?	**No, I can't.**

① Match the questions with the responses.

1 Can you dance?

2 Can you fly a kite?

3 Can you ride a horse?

4 Can you stand on one leg?

5 Can you play the guitar?

6 Can you swim?

a I don't know. Let's see. Woah! No, I can't.

b Yes, I can. I can play the piano, too.

c Yes, I can, and I can sing.

d No, I can't. I haven't got a kite.

e Yes, I can. I swim at the weekends.

f No, I can't, but I can ride a bike.

2 **Complete the sentences with the words from the box.**

sing   speak   play   can   ~~Yes~~   can't

Karl   Hello, May. Can you dance?

May   **(1)** __Yes__ , I can.

Karl   Can you **(2)** _____ the guitar?

May   No, I **(3)** _____ . But I can play the piano
and I can **(4)** _____ .

Karl   Can you **(5)** _____ Spanish?

May   No, I can't. But my sister **(6)** _____ .

3 **Write questions.**

1 (piano) __Can you play the piano?__

No, I can't. But I can play the guitar.

2 (speak Spanish) _____

Yes, I can. ¡Hola!

3 (play tennis) _____

No, I can't. I can play football.

4 (ride a bike) _____

Yes, I can. My bike is pink.

5 (swim) _____

Yes, I can.

6 (ride a horse) _____

No, I can't. I don't like horses.

Reading: a forum

1 Read the text and the sentences. Write *yes* or *no*.

Pet forum

Super pets!

Alice

Can your cat sing?!

My cat is called Bob. He's black with one white foot! He's two years old. He can run and jump AND he can sing! What can your pet do?

Harry

Wow! No way! My cat can't sing. I've got a dog, too. His name is Patch. He can swim and he can play football – we play football in the garden! Look at my photo.

Sally

Cool! I haven't got a cat or a dog, but I've got a horse. Her name is Jazzy. She's a big black horse – she's beautiful. She can't sing. She can jump up high, stand on two legs and she can skip.

1 Bob is one.   **no**

2 Bob can't sing.   _____

3 Patch can swim.   _____

4 Patch can't play football.   _____

5 Jazzy is ugly.   _____

6 Jazzy can skip and jump.   _____

1 **Choose a pet and make notes.**

Pet _____

What's her/his name? _____

What colour is she/he? _____

How old is she/he? _____

She/he can _____

She/he can't _____

2 **Write a forum post. Use your notes from Activity 1 to help you.**

● ● ●

Pet forum

Super pets!

_____

_____

_____

_____

_____

_____

_____

_____

1 🎧 17 Listen and colour.

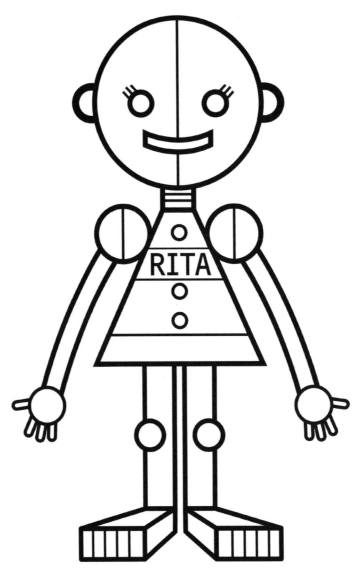

2 🎧 18 What can Rita do? Listen and tick ☑ or cross ☒.

What can Rita do?

talk ☑   jump ☐

walk ☐   dance ☐

run ☐   sing ☐

1 **Ask and answer.**
Use the words from the box.

Can you touch your toes?

Yes, I can.

skip   make   fly   touch   swim   play   sing

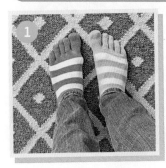

2 **Imagine and draw a robot. Complete and practise.**

This is my robot. Her/His name's
_____. My robot can
_____, _____
and _____. My robot can't
_____ or _____.

3 **Talk about your robot.**

This is my robot. His name's Rob. Rob can talk, sing and skip. Rob can't dance or swim.

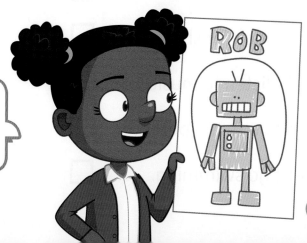

75

9 Suggestions

Language focus

Use **Let's + verb** to make suggestions.

	Good idea.
Let's play *the guitar.*	*I'm not sure.*
	Sorry, I don't want to.

1 **Match the sentences with the pictures.**

1 Let's paint a picture. ☑ d

2 Let's take a photo. ☐

3 Let's look for shells. ☐

4 Let's listen to music. ☐

5 Let's go to the park. ☐

6 Let's go swimming. ☐

2 Complete the sentences with the words from the box.

~~Let's~~ idea play sure eat want

Hugo **(1)** ___Let's___ look for shells.

Tony I'm not **(2)** _____.

Hugo OK. Let's **(3)** _____ football.

Tony Sorry, I don't **(4)** _____ to – we haven't got a ball.

Hugo Let's **(5)** _____ an ice cream.

Tony Good **(6)** _____. Banana is my favourite ice cream!

3 Look and write.

1 Let's play the guitar.
✓ ___Good idea.___

2 _____
✗ Sorry, _____.

3 _____
✓ _____

4 _____
✗ I'm _____.

5 _____
✗ I'm _____.

6 _____
✓ _____

Where's / Where are ... ?

> Where's the red T-shirt?

> It's on the bed.

> Where are the green shoes?

> They're under the bed.

> Where are the black shorts?

> They're in the bag.

> Thanks Mum!

Language focus

Use **Where's ... ?** to ask about singular items.
Use **It's ...** to answer about singular items.

Use **Where are ... ?** to ask about plural items.
Use **They're ...** to answer about plural items.

Where's *the blue book?*   **It's** *in the green bag.*

Where are *the orange books?*   **They're** *in the black bag.*

---

1 **Write the questions.**

1 are / Where / small / the / shells / ?   Where are the small shells?

2 is / the / dog / Where / big / ? _____

3 are / blue / shoes / the / Where / ? _____

4 the / Where / is / cat / ? _____

5 beach / the / Where / is / ? _____

6 orange / Where / the / are / kites / ? _____

2 Look and write answers.

1 Where's the blue book?

   It's in the green bag.

2 Where's the green lizard?

_____

3 Where are the green books?

_____

4 Where's the purple spider?

_____

5 Where are the red books?

_____

6 Where's the yellow lizard?

_____

3 Look. Complete the questions and answers.

1 Where 's the lizard ?

   It's _____ in the bedroom.

2 _____ the crocodiles?

   _____ in the bathroom.

3 _____ the cat?

   _____ room.

4 _____ the spider?

   _____

5 _____ ?

It's in the cellar.

Reading: a magazine

1 Read the text and answer the questions.

Come to Wales

Wales is a beautiful country. There are lots of places to see. You can walk in the high mountains and swim in the sea at the beautiful beaches. There are lots of mountains, but go to Snowdon mountain. It's really high, so take your walking shoes! There are also lots of castles. Go to famous Conwy Castle – it's very old. You can walk to the top of the castle and take photos of the mountains and the sea. You can see sheep, too! Have lunch in the Castle café and eat Welsh cakes! Wales is fantastic!

Welsh cakes

Conwy Castle

1 What adjectives can you find? What do they describe?
__beautiful country__ _____ _____ _____ _____

2 What activities can you do on holiday in Wales?
_____ _____ _____

3 What is the name of the high mountain? _____

4 What can you do at Conwy castle?
_____

5 What animals can you see from the castle? _____

6 What food can you try? _____

1 Match the phrases.

1 walk up Ben Nevis   a bagpipe music

2 go to Edinburgh   b the Loch Ness monster

3 listen to   c haggis (meat with onion)

4 eat   d a mountain

5 look for shells on   e a city

6 find   f the fantastic beaches

2 Write a magazine article about Scotland. Use the phrases in Activity 1 to help you.

_____

_____

_____

_____

_____

_____

_____

_____

Listening: holidays

1 🎧 **19** Listen and tick ☑ the correct picture.

2 🎧 **20** Listen and draw lines.

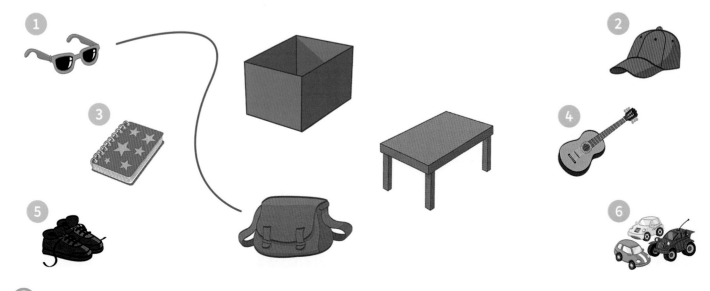

1 **You want to take these things on holiday. Where are they? Choose and circle.**

1 My T-shirts are *in my bag / on the table.*

2 My sunglasses are *on the table / on the chair.*

3 My guitar is *in the toy box / under the table.*

4 My books are *in my bag / on the table.*

5 My kite is *in the toy box / under the chair.*

6 My shorts are *on the chair / under the table.*

2 **Ask your friend about the things in Activity 1. Tick ☑.**

> Where are your T-shirts?

> They're on the table.

	🎒	🪑(table)	🪑(chair)	📦
1 T-shirts				
2 sunglasses				
3 guitar				
4 books				
5 kite				
6 shorts				

3 **With your friend, choose and colour five activities for your holiday. Then say.**

> Let's catch a fish.

> I'm not sure. Let's look for shells.

> OK. Good idea!

| catch a fish | take photos | read a book | paint pictures |

| make sandcastles | swim in the sea | eat ice cream |

| look for shells | listen to music | play the guitar |

Audioscripts

Welcome Unit page 10

Sam: Hello! I'm Sam. What's your name?
Ana: I'm Ana. How old are you, Sam?
Sam: I'm eight. How old are you, Ana?
Ana: I'm seven.

Kim: Hi!
Dan: Hello!
Kim: I'm Kim. What's your name?
Dan: I'm Dan.
Kim: What a nice name! How old are you, Dan?
Dan: I'm six. How old are you, Kim?
Kim: I'm nine.

Sam: I'm Sam. My hat is red.
Ana: I'm Ana. Look! My balloon is blue.
Dan: I'm Dan. My bag is green.
Kim: I'm Kim. Look! My balloon is orange.

Unit 1 page 18

03

1 **Teacher:** What's this?
  Girl: It's a pencil case. It's green.
  Teacher: Yes, it's my pencil case!
2 **Boy:** Hmm. Is it a pen?
  Girl: No, it isn't. It's a pencil.
  Boy: OK. What colour is it?
  Girl: It's blue.
3 **Girl:** What's this?
  Boy: It's a ruler.
  Girl: Yes, it is! It's your ruler!
4 **Boy:** Is it a book?
  Teacher: No, it isn't.
  Boy: Oh, it's a notebook!
  Teacher: Yes, it is.

5 **Girl:** What's this?
  Teacher: It's paper.
6 **Boy:** Look at my bag – it's purple.
  Girl: Wow! It's cool!

04

Open your pencil case, please. Now get a pencil. Look at this box, please. Now write your name on the box! And now … Put away your pencil, please.

Unit 2 page 26

05

1 **Boy:** What's this?
  Girl: It's my favourite toy. My doll.
  Boy: Oh, it's a beautiful doll!
  Girl: Thank you! Her name's Lulu.
2 **Girl:** How old are you?
  Boy: I'm seven.
  Girl: And how old is your friend Daniel?
  Boy: He's eight.
3 **Girl:** Look at this big blue monster!
  Boy: His name's Zak!
  Girl: Zak is ugly!
  Boy: Yes, but he's my favourite toy!
4 **Boy:** What's her name?
  Girl: Sara. She's my friend.
  Boy: How old is she?
  Girl: She's six.
  Boy: And what's her favourite toy?
  Girl: Her favourite toy's her new yellow kite.

06

Hi! My name's Oliver. My friend's name's Emma. She's seven. These are her favourite toys. Look! This is her big yellow ball. Yellow is Emma's favourite colour. And this is her pink plane. It's new! And can you see the small green car? It's my favourite toy, too! Oh no, it isn't … It's the long blue train!

Unit 3 page 34

1 Boy: Oh, no! My frog isn't here.
Girl: Look! Your frog's on your notebook!
2 Girl: My duck? It's not in the pond …
Where is it?
Boy: It's there! Look – under the chair.
3 Ben: Look, May – a spider!
May: A spider? Where?
Ben: On the box!
May: *In* the box?
Ben: No! *On* the box – there!
May: Oh, yes! I can see it now.
4 May: Ben, where's the cat?
Ben: The cat? Well, it's not under the tree …
Oh, look – it's in the hat!
May: The cat's in the hat!

Jill: Hey, Bill. Let's look at these pictures of animals. Look – a dog. I like dogs.
What about you?
Bill: Hmm, I don't like dogs, Jill.
Jill: Oh, a lizard! I don't like lizards – they're ugly!
Bill: Ugly? Come on, Jill. Lizards are cool.
I like lizards!
Jill: Oh, look at this donkey. I like donkeys.
What about you, Bill?
Bill: I like donkeys too, Jill!
Jill: Hey, an elephant! I like elephants!
Bill: Me too! I like elephants – they're my favourite!
Jill: Hmm, what's this, Bill?
Bill: It's a spider!
Jill: A spider? Oh, no! I don't like spiders!
Bill: I know. And I don't like spiders, Jill!

Unit 4 page 42

Hello! I'm Laura and it's my birthday! I'm seven today. Look – this is the food for my birthday: I've got cheese sandwiches – they're my favourite! And I've got sausages and … oh, yes! A pizza. I've got a big pizza for my friends. I like apples, but I haven't got apples today – I've got bananas. Big yellow bananas. I haven't got chicken and I haven't got carrots. Oh! But I've got a beautiful cake – my birthday cake! Yummy!

1 Leo: I'm hungry, Rose. Have we got any cheese?
Rose: No, we haven't, Leo. We've got peas!
Leo: Peas? Oh, no! I don't like peas …
2 Nick: Mum, have we got any fish for lunch?
Mum: Yes, Nick, we have. Here's the fish.
You're hungry!
3 Boy: OK, Ann, have we got any cheese for the pizza?
Ann: Let's see … Oh, no, we haven't.
Boy: Yes, we have. Look – this is cheese.
Ann: Oh, yes! Yummy!
4 Tina: Mmm, Dad, is this for lunch?
Dad: Yes, Tina. We've got a big steak – your favourite!
Tina: Yes, it is! Thanks, Dad.

Unit 5 page 50

Tess: Hi! I'm Tess and I play the piano. I play the piano on Wednesdays.
Peter: Hello! My name's Peter. I like TV! I watch TV on Saturdays. Saturday's my favourite day!
Holly: Hello! I'm Holly and I play football. Football is great! I play football on Fridays.
Jack: Hi! I'm Jack. I like Mondays. I go swimming on Mondays!
Anna: Hi! My name's Anna. I play with my toys on Sundays. Yes, I play with my teddy and my doll on Sundays.
James: Hello! I'm James and I like my bike. I ride my bike on … Thursdays … Oh, no! Not on Thursdays, on Tuesdays. That's right. I ride my bike on Tuesdays.

Woman: Hi, Jane! I've got a question for you. What do you do at the weekend?

Jane: Well, I do lots of things!

Woman: Do you play tennis?

Jane: Yes, I do. I play tennis on Fridays.

Woman: Do you go swimming on Fridays, too?

Jane: No, I don't. I go swimming on Saturdays. And I play games with my family on Saturdays.

Woman: That's nice – do you play computer games?

Jane: No, board games.

Woman: Great! I like board games.

Jane: Me too! Oh, and on Sundays I ride my bike. I've got a new bike!

Woman: Fantastic! And do you play football on Sundays, too?

Jane: No, I don't. I don't like football.

Woman: OK, that's all. Thanks, Jane!

Unit 6 page 58

1 Look! There's a monster in the bedroom.

2 Now, the kitchen – there are two monsters. There are two monsters in the kitchen.

3 I can see a monster on the stairs. There's a monster on the stairs!

4 Look! There's a monster in the bathroom.

5 Can you see the hall? There are two monsters in the hall.

6 And now, the living room – there are two monsters in the living room.

Mr Smith: OK, Amy. Tell us about your house. How many rooms are there?

Amy: Hmm. One, two … There are eight rooms. We've got eight rooms, Mr Smith.

Mr Smith: Hmm! There are *seven* rooms in *my* house. And how many bedrooms are there?

Amy: There are three bedrooms. Three bedrooms, and two bathrooms.

Mr Smith: OK. And is there a garden?

Amy: No, there isn't. There isn't a garden, but there's a cool park near my house.

Mr Smith: That's nice! Now, is there a desk in your bedroom?

Amy: No, there isn't. My bedroom's small. But there's a big desk in the living room. And it's for me!

Mr Smith: Great! Now, the last question – are there any stairs in your house?

Amy: No, there aren't. My house is big, but there aren't any stairs.

Mr Smith: OK! Thanks, Amy!

Unit 7 page 66

🎧 15

1 **Boy:** Do you like these socks?
  Girl: Yes, I do.
  Boy: Me too!

2 **Girl:** Do you like this jacket?
  Boy: Yes, I like your jacket. You look good like that.
  Girl: Thanks!

3 **Boy:** Do you like these trousers?
  Girl: Hmm … No, I don't. They're ugly.

4 **Girl:** Do you like these shoes?
  Boy: Hmm … No, I don't. I don't like the colour.

5 **Boy:** Look at this sweater! Do you like it?
  Girl: Yes, I do. It's nice!

6 **Girl:** I like this T-shirt. What about you?
  Boy: Oh, yes, I like it, too!

🎧 16

Eric: Look, Dad! My friends are in the park!

Dad: Where, Eric?

Eric: There! Look, that's Stan. He's playing with the ball.

Dad: Oh! Is he wearing a red T-shirt?

Eric: Yes, he is. And look, that's Oscar! Oscar's wearing a blue baseball cap.

Dad: OK. I can see Oscar now. I like his cap!

Eric: Me too! Oh, and that's Stella – she's riding her bike.

Dad: Hmm. Is she wearing shorts?

Eric: Yes, she is. She's wearing orange shorts.

Dad: Oh, and is that Lucy?

Eric: No, Dad. That's Maya. Maya's wearing jeans, and Lucy's wearing a purple skirt.

Dad: Oh, I can see now. Lucy's wearing a purple skirt.

Eric: Yes, that's right!

Unit 8 page 74

 17

Hi! My name's Rita and I'm a robot! This is my head – I've got a big yellow head. And look! I've got two hands – one and two. My hands are orange. Now, these are my arms. I've got long arms! They're purple. I've got purple toes, too! I've got ten purple toes. And can you see these? They're my knees. I've got two blue knees. I like blue!

 18

Ellie: Look, Jack. This is my new robot, Rita.

Jack: Wow! She's cool! I like her long arms.

Ellie: Me too! She's great. She can talk! Listen.

Robot: Hi! My name's Rita.

Jack: That's nice. Can she walk, too?

Ellie: Yes, Rita can walk. Look!

Jack: Fantastic! Hey! Can Rita run?

Ellie: Er … No, she can't. Rita can walk, but she can't run.

Jack: That's OK.

Ellie: Oh! But she can jump! Look at this.

Jack: Cool!

Ellie: And … She can dance! Look!

Jack: Hahaha, that's amazing! Hey! Can Rita dance *and* sing?

Ellie: Hmm … No, she can't sing … But you and I can! Come on!

Jack: All right, Ellie! You know I can't sing … But I can play with Rita!

Unit 9 page 82

 19

1 Ben: We're at the beach!

Sara: Hurrah! Let's swim in the sea!

Ben: Hmm … Sorry, I don't want to. Let's make a sandcastle.

Sara: OK. Good idea.

2 Ben: Sara! Let's fly the kites!

Sara: Oh, I haven't got my kite. I'm hungry … Let's eat an ice cream!

Ben: Mmm! Good idea!

3 Sara: Let's play tennis, Ben.

Ben: Tennis? At the beach? I'm not sure …

Sara: You're right! We can't play tennis here. Let's look for shells.

Ben: OK!

4 Ben: Sara, where's my book?

Sara: It's at home, Ben.

Ben: Oh … OK. Let's play the guitar, then.

Sara: Great idea! Here's the guitar.

5 Sara: Ben, look at this fish!

Ben: Wow! It's beautiful! Let's take a photo.

Sara: Good idea!

 20

1 Mary: Mum, where are my sunglasses? They aren't on the table.

Mum: They're in your bag.

Mary: OK. Thanks, Mum!

2 Mary: Dad, where's my baseball cap?

Dad: Hmm … It isn't in your bag.

Mary: Oh, it's here. It's on the table.

3 Mum: Mary, your notebook isn't on the table. Where is it?

Mary: My notebook? It's in my bag, Mum.

Mum: OK, great.

4 Dad: Let's play the guitar. Oh, but … where's my guitar?

Mum: The guitar's on the table, Daniel.

Dad: OK, thanks, Sue!

5 Mary: My shoes aren't here … Where are they?

Mum: Look! They're in the box!

Mary: In the box? Oh, yes, they are!

6 Mary: Dad, are my cars on the table?

Dad: No, they aren't, Mary. Look – they're in the box.

Mary: Cool! Thanks, Dad.

Acknowledgements

The authors and publishers acknowledge the following sources of copyright material and are grateful for the permissions granted. While every effort has been made, it has not always been possible to identify the sources of all the material used, or to trace all copyright holders. If any omissions are brought to our notice, we will be happy to include the appropriate acknowledgements on reprinting and in the next update to the digital edition, as applicable.

Key: U = Unit

Photography

The following images are sourced from Getty Images.

U1: Lemon_tm/iStock/Getty Images Plus; jesadaphorn/iStock/Getty Images Plus; t_kimura/E+; urfinguss/iStock/Getty Images Plus; **U2**: Ismailciydem/iStock/Getty Images Plus; **U3**: MmeEmil/E+; ozgurdonmaz/iStock/Getty Images Plus; Divesh_Mistry/iStock/Getty Images Plus; Smitt/iStock/Getty Images Plus; GlobalP/iStock/Getty Images Plus; 2happy/iStock/Getty Images Plus; photographer, loves art, lives in Kyoto/Moment; Arathrael Photography/Moment; Ulianna /iStock/Getty Images plus; **U4**: Wavebreakmedia Ltd/Wavebreak Media; Jose Luis Pelaez Inc/DigitalVision; Juanmonino/E+; vfoto/iStock/Getty Images Plus; milanfoto/E+; gbh007/iStock/Getty Images Plus; etiennevoss/iStock/Getty Images Plus; **U5**: bowie15/iStock/Getty Images Plus; SDI Productions/E+; Fancy/Veer/Corbis; Asia Images/Photodisc; Big Cheese Photo; Icealien/iStock/Getty Images Plus; Tigatelu/iStock/Getty Images plus; **U7**: Issaurinko/iStock/Getty Images Plus; NYS444/iStock/Getty Images Plus; heinteh/iStock/Getty Images Plus; Olga Gillmeister/iStock/Getty Images Plus; Ng Sok Lian/EyeEm; mustafagull/iStock/Getty Images Plus; ValuaVitaly/iStock/Getty Images Plus; somethingway/iStock/Getty Images Plus; KathyDewar/iStock/Getty Images Plus; JudyKennamer/iStock/Getty Images Plus; Steve Prezant/Image Source; Compassionate Eye Foundation/DigitalVision; **U8**: Studio Light and Shade/iStock/Getty Images Plus; Creative Crop/Photodisc; viafilms/iStock/Getty Images Plus; popovaphoto/iStock/Getty Images Plus; Richard Coombs/EyeEm; ThePROmax/iStock/Getty Images Plus; JasonDoiy/iStock/Getty Images Plus; scanrail/iStock/Getty Images Plus; Steve Prezant/Image Source; Ami-Rian/iStock/Getty Images plus; kenex/DigitalVision Vectors; alexei_tm/iStock/Getty Images plus; **U9**: photoguns/iStock/Getty Images Plus; Firmafotografen/iStock/Getty Images Plus; tulcarion/E+; aedkais/iStock/Getty Images Plus; Joff Lee/Photolibrary; Mariusz Kluzniak/Moment Open.

The following images are sourced from other sources/libraries.

U1: spaxiax/Shutterstock; duckycards/iStockphoto; Tpopova/iStockphoto; oku/Shutterstock; Mosutatsu/iStockphoto; EuToch/iStockphoto; **U8**: tkemot/Shutterstock; Alex White/Shutterstock; Cybernesco/iStockphoto; Riddy/iStockphoto; carlosalvarez/iStockphoto; Mike Flippo/Shutterstock.

Commissioned photography by Stephen Bond.

Illustrations

Anna Hancock (Beehive); Alan Rowe; Bernice Lum; Chris Lensch; Clive Goodyer; Daniel Limon; David Semple; Marek Jagucki.

Audio

All the audio clips are sourced from Getty Images.

FRANCIS CERIONI/Sound Effects; Jupiter Images/Sound Effects; Sound Effects; Mirko Pernjakovic/Sound Effects; Michael Harrison/Sound Effects; Rok Stibler/Sound Effects; Cedric Hommel/Sound Effects; LDj_Audio/Sound Effects.

Audio produced by Hart McLeod.

Typeset

EMC Design limited.

Cover design by We Are Bold.